The sawfish cuts up other fish into bite-size pieces with the sharp, toothed edges of its snout.

The parrotfish's teeth grow together to make a beak like a bird's, which it uses to bite into coral.

The flounder is a nearly flat fish that lies on the sandy bottom of inlets and bays. Both of its eyes look up from the same side of its head.

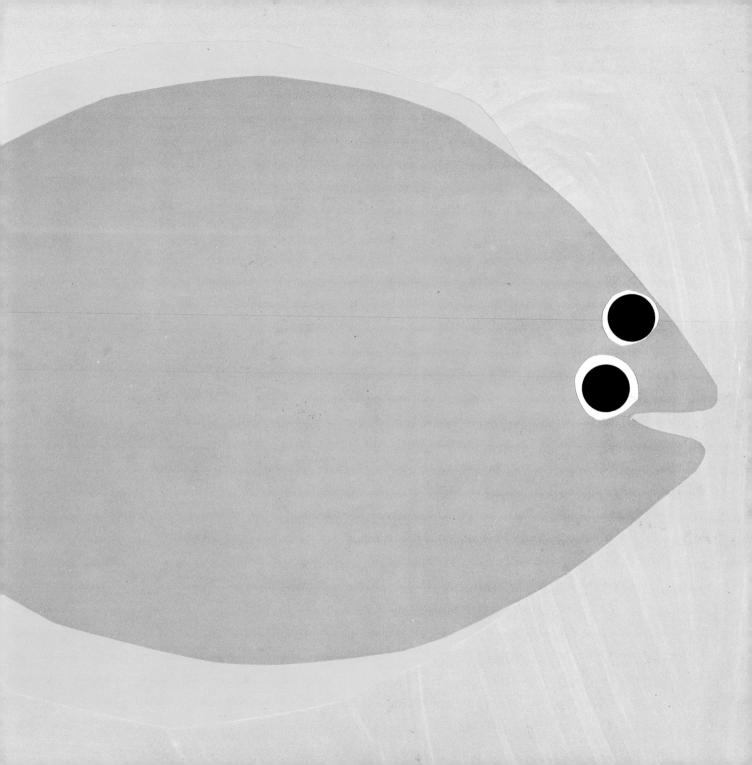

The electric eel moves backward or forward, up or down.

Muscles in its long tail make electricity, which it uses to stun prey.

The goosefish has a mouth
that is nearly as wide as its body.
A lure hangs from a spine
in front of its teeth to
attract small fish.

As they put their mouths together
and appear to kiss, grunts grind their teeth
and make piglike noises.

The hammerhead shark
swims quickly
as it chases its prey.

Its eyes are far
apart on the sides
of its head.

The butterfly fish has an "eyespot" near its tail that makes it hard for other fish to tell its head from its tail.

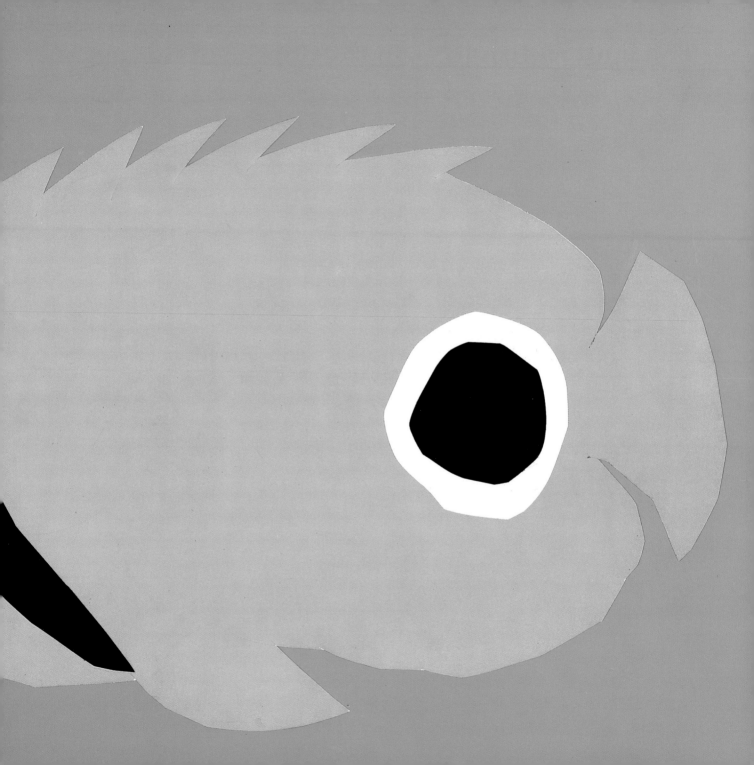

The lantern fish lives in the depths of the sea during the day, but rises to the surface at night.

The spots along its body
glow in the dark.

**With tiny side fins and a little tail,
the cowfish is a very slow swimmer.**

When the puffer
is afraid, it swallows
lots of water or air
and blows itself up
into a prickly ball
too large for most
other fish to swallow.

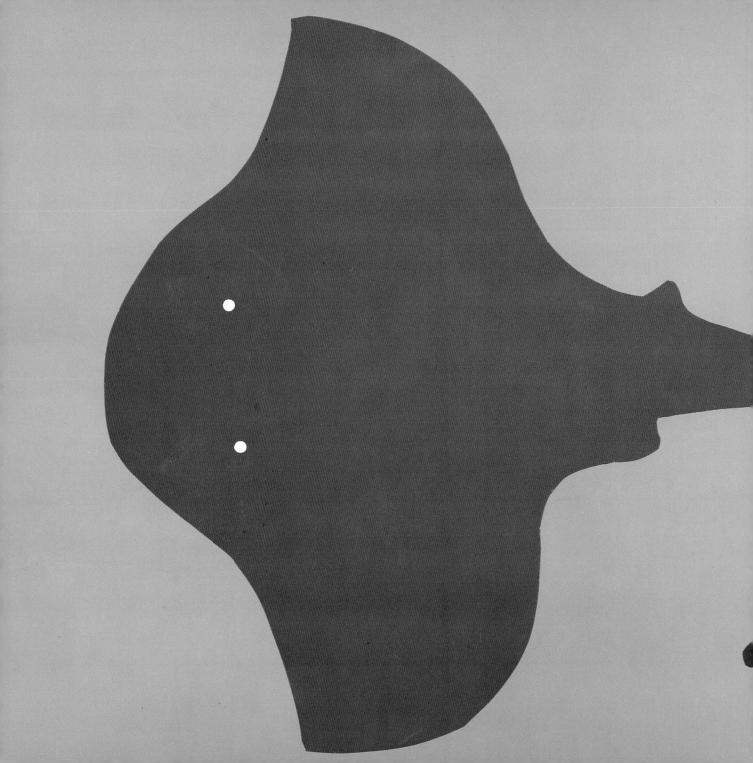

The stingray has a stinger on its long, thin tail.
It rests on the bottom of the ocean,
hidden in the sand, and only stings if it
is disturbed or frightened.

After

a mother sea horse

lays her eggs,

the father sea horse

carries them

in his pouch

until they hatch

and the babies

swim out.